LEGENDS AND FABLES PAPERCRAFTS

Written and illustrated by

Jerome C. Brown

Fearon Teacher Aids
Simon & Schuster Supplementary Education Group

Editor: Carol Williams
Copyeditor: Kristin Eclov
Design: Diann Abbott

ISBN 0-8224-4234-5
Printed in the United States of America

1. 9 8 7 6 5 4 3 2 1

CONTENTS

INTRODUCTION

This book contains directions and patterns for making masks, stick puppets, watercolor paintings, and other papercraft projects to enhance the enjoyment of fables and legends from around the world. Most of the stories can be found in your local library in a book bearing the title's name. "How the Camel Got His Hump" can be found in *Just So Stories* by Rudyard Kipling. The last three titles in the contents can be found in a collection of Aesop's fables. Read each story aloud to your class with expression and enthusiasm before beginning the papercraft projects.

Organizational Helps

Construction paper is used in each papercraft. It is referred to as art paper in the list of materials that accompanies each project. Colors of art paper are suggested but can be changed to suit your needs. Since you will need a pencil, ruler, scissors, glue, and markers or crayons for each project, these items are not listed in each materials list.

For each art project children enjoy, the teacher must spend time in preparation and gathering supplies. This book was designed to minimize that time. Stick puppets are frequently used throughout this book. A special dotted line has been drawn around the figures to make cutting easier for younger children. Older children can ignore the dotted line and cut out the intricate details of the figures.

Uses for Papercrafts

A coloring page is the first activity listed for each story. Invite children to staple the coloring pages together in a book with a sheet of writing paper between each coloring page. Encourage children to write a story summary, a different ending, or rewrite their favorite part of each story following the coloring page. Or, children can research information about the country from which each legend or fable comes and write down some interesting facts.

Plays and skits can be designed around the masks and puppets. Assign different characters to students and group them to create dialogue and practice a reenactment of the legend or fable. Older children may enjoy making the projects and presenting a skit to a younger group of children.

Display the projects on a mural or bulletin board. Invite the students to create a background with chalk or paint. It is the author's hope that these papercrafts will allow you to bring literature to life in your classroom.

Why the Crab Has No Head (Africa)

Why the Crab Has No Head (Animal Stick Puppets)

Materials

- Patterns on pages 7-9 reproduced on white art paper
- White art paper 9" x 12" (22.9 cm x 30.5 cm)
- Tongue depressor or popsicle stick for each puppet

Procedure

1. Color patterns using crayons or markers.

2. Place white art paper behind pattern pages and cut patterns out to produce two copies. (Or patterns can be cut out and then traced and recut on the white art paper.)

3. Place a tongue depressor or popsicle stick between the patterns and glue the two pieces together. Allow the stick to extend enough to make a comfortable handle (figs. A and B).

Figure A

Figure B

Elephant

Lion

Why the Crab Has No Head (Stick Puppets)   7

Lizard

Crocodile

Why the Crab Has No Head (Stick Puppets)

Leopard

Turtle

Guineafowl

Legend of the Milky Way (China)

Legends and Fables Papercrafts © 1991 Fearon Teacher Aids

Legend of the Milky Way
(Stick Puppets)

Materials

- Patterns on pages 12-15 reproduced on white art paper
- White art paper 9" x 12" (22.9 cm x 30.5 cm)
- Tongue depressor or popsicle stick for each puppet

Procedure

1. Color patterns using crayons or markers.

2. Place white art paper behind pattern pages and cut patterns out to produce two copies. (Or patterns can be cut out and then traced and recut on the white art paper.)

3. Place a tongue depressor or popsicle stick between the patterns and glue the two pieces together. Allow the stick to extend enough to make a comfortable handle (figs. A and B).

4. Use an X-acto knife to cut eyeholes in the water buffalo mask (fig. C).

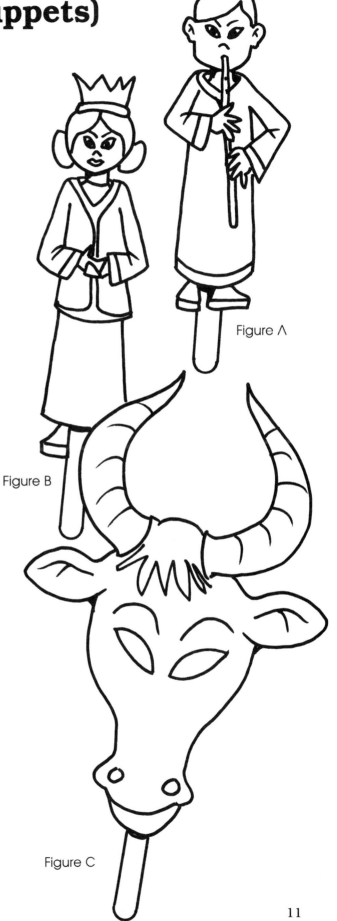

Figure A

Figure B

Figure C

Legend of the Milky Way (Water Buffalo Mask)

King of the Heavens

Queen Mother

Legend of the Milky Way (Stick Puppets)   13

Guard

Boy with Flute

14   **Legend of the Milky Way (Stick Puppets)**

Weaver Princess

Young Man

The Pied Piper of Hamelin (Germany)

The Pied Piper of Hamelin (Hats)

Materials

Stapler

Art Paper (Hat 1):
- Brown 12" x 18" (30.5 cm x 45.7 cm) cone-shaped hat
- Yellow 3" x 12" (7.6 cm x 30.5 cm) feather
- Red 1" x 18" (2.5 cm x 45.7 cm) hat strip

Art Paper (Hat 2):
- Red 18" x 24" (45.7 cm x 61 cm) hat
- Yellow 3" x 12" (7.6 cm x 30.5 cm) feather

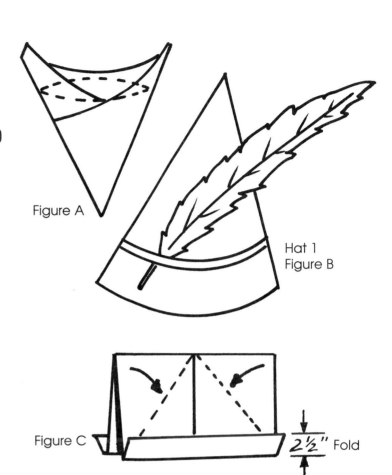

Figure A

Hat 1
Figure B

Procedure

1. For Hat 1, staple the brown art paper into a cone 6 1/2" in diameter. Trim edges (fig. A).

2. Staple or glue red strip around hat.

3. Trace and cut out yellow feather. Glue feather in place (fig.B).

4. For Hat 2, fold red art paper in half widthwise. Fold each end up 2 1/2". Fold both corners down to meet the base of the hat inside the 2 1/2" tab (fig. C).

5. Fold the corners down on one end of the hat and staple to create a point. Round the other corners and staple (fig. D).

6. Trace and cut out the yellow feather. Glue feather in place (fig. E).

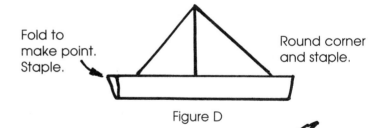

Figure C

2½" Fold

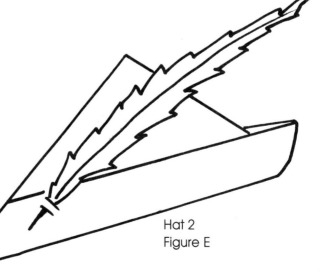

Fold to make point. Staple.

Round corner and staple.

Figure D

Hat 2
Figure E

feather

yellow

The Pied Piper of Hamelin (Hat Feather)

The Pied Piper of Hamelin
(Rat Stick Puppets)

Materials

- Patterns on page 20 reproduced on gray art paper
- Gray art paper 9" x 12" (22.9 cm x 30.5 cm)
- Tongue depressor or popsicle stick for each puppet
- Two plastic eyes for each puppet
- Gray pipe cleaner for each puppet

Procedure

1. Color patterns using crayons or markers.

2. Place gray art paper behind pattern page and cut patterns out to produce two copies. (Or patterns can be cut out and then traced and recut on the white art paper.)

3. Place a tongue depressor or popsicle stick between the patterns and glue the two pieces together. Allow the stick to extend enough to make a comfortable handle (figs. A and B).

4. Glue pipe cleaner in place for the rat's tail and add plastic eyes.

Figure A

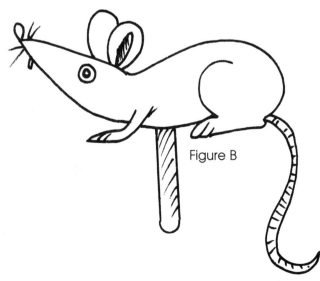

Figure B

The Pied Piper of Hamelin (Rat Stick Puppets)

How the Camel Got His Hump (India)

How the Camel Got His Hump (Djinn Stick Puppet)

Materials

- Pattern on page 23 reproduced on white art paper
- White art paper 9" x 12" (22.9 cm x 30.5 cm)
- Tongue depressor or popsicle stick

Procedure

1. Color patterns using crayons or markers.

2. Place white art paper behind pattern page and cut pattern out to produce two copies. (Or pattern can be cut out and then traced and recut on the white art paper.)

3. Place a tongue depressor or popsicle stick between the patterns and glue the two pieces together. Allow the stick to extend enough to make a comfortable handle (fig. A).

Figure A

Legends and Fables Papercrafts © 1991 Fearon Teacher Aids

How the Camel Got His Hump (Animal Jointed Puppets)

Materials

- Brass fasteners
- Patterns on pages 25-28 reproduced on art paper listed below

Art Paper:

- Gray 9" x 12" (22.9 cm x 30.5 cm) camel
- Dark brown 9" x 12" (22.9 cm x 30.5 cm) horse
- Light brown 9" x 12" (22.9 cm x 30.5 cm) ox
- White 9" x 12" (22.9 cm x 30.5 cm) dog

Procedure

1. Color the pattern pieces or add details with crayons or markers.
2. Cut out patterns. Patterns can be glued to tagboard to give them more stability.
3. Stick brass fasteners through the designated holes to connect the pattern pieces (figs. A, B, C, and D).

Figure A

Figure B

Figure C

Figure D

Legends and Fables Papercrafts © 1991 Fearon Teacher Aids

hump

body

tail

hind legs

front legs

How the Camel Got His Hump (Camel)

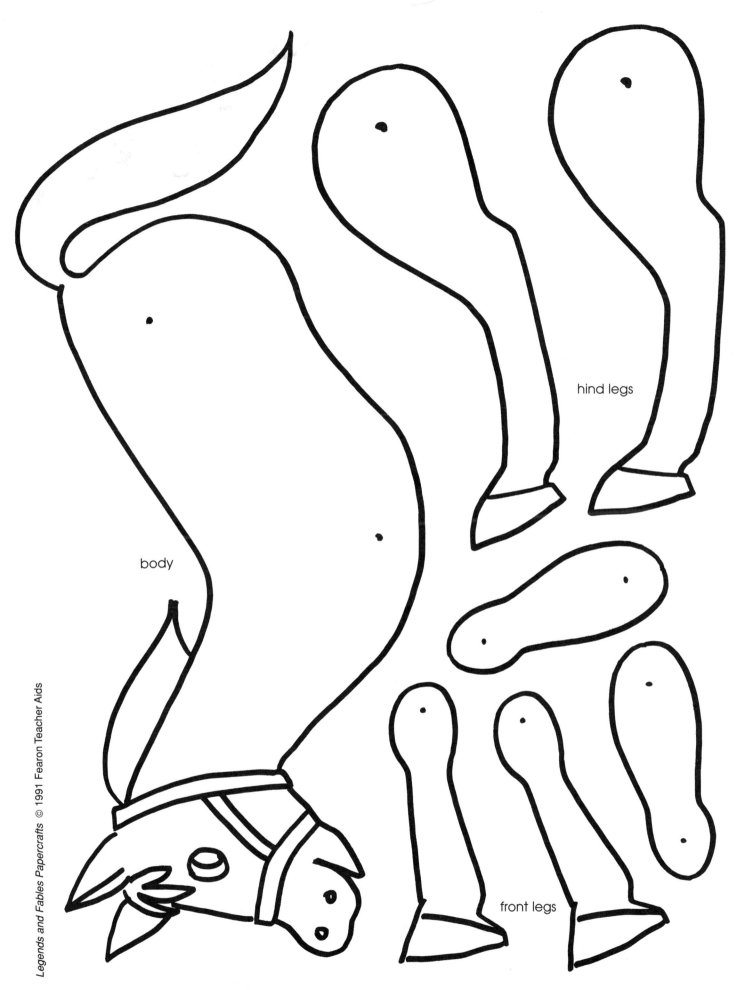

body

hind legs

front legs

How the Camel Got His Hump (Horse) 27

yoke

body

front legs

hind legs

How the Camel Got His Hump (Ox)

Little One Inch (Japan)

Little One Inch
(Stick Puppet and Masks)

Materials

- Patterns on pages 31-38 reproduced on white art paper
- White art paper 9" x 12" (22.9 cm x 30.5 cm)
- Tongue depressor or popsicle stick for each mask or puppet

Procedure

1. Color patterns using crayons or markers.

2. Place white art paper behind pattern pages and cut patterns out to produce two copies. (Or pattern can be cut out and then traced and recut on the white art paper.)

3. Place a tongue depressor or popsicle stick between the patterns and glue the two pieces together. Allow the stick to extend enough to make a comfortable handle (fig. A).

4. Use an X-acto knife to cut eyeholes in each mask (fig. B).

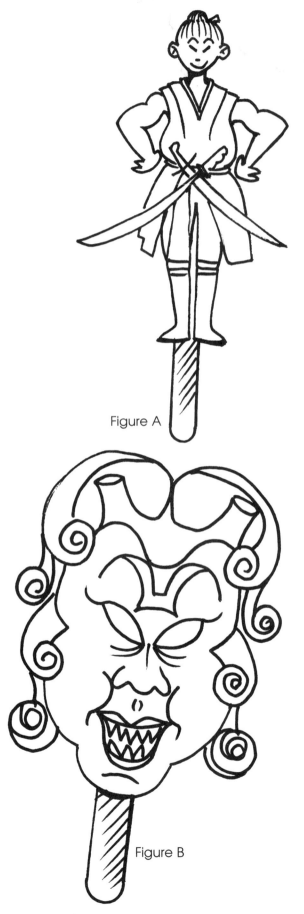

Figure A

Figure B

30

Legends and Fables Papercrafts © 1991 Fearon Teacher Aids

Little One Inch (Farmer Mask)   31

Little One Inch (Wife Mask)

Little One Inch (Issun Boshi Stick Puppet)

Little One Inch (Kappa Mask)

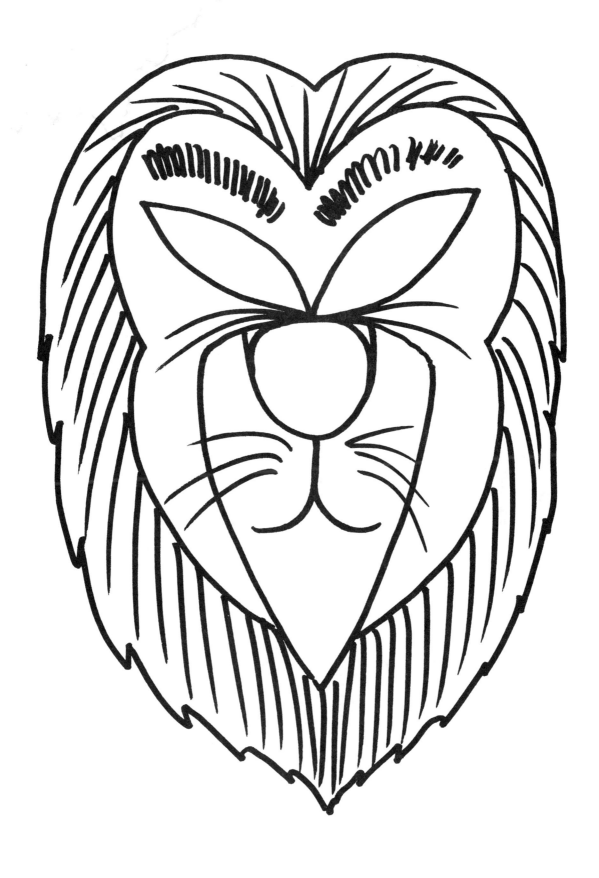

Little One Inch (Tengu Mask) 35

Little One Inch (Merchant Mask)

Little One Inch (Michiko Mask)   37

Little One Inch (Horned Giant Mask)

Legends and Fables Papercrafts © 1991 Fearon Teacher Aids

The Legend of Scarface
(Native American)

The Legend of Scarface (Scarface, Singing Rains, Wolf, and Bear Masks)

Materials

- Tongue depressor or popsicle stick for each mask
- Patterns on pages 41-44 reproduced on art paper

Art Paper:

- Two white 9" x 12" (22.9 cm x 30.5 cm) Scarface
- Two white 9" x 12" (22.9 cm x 30.5 cm) Singing Rains
- Two gray 9" x 12" (22.9 cm x 30.5 cm) wolf
- Two brown 9" x 12" (22.9 cm x 30.5 cm) bear

Procedure

1. Color patterns or add details using crayons or markers.

2. Place second sheet of 9" x 12" (22.9 cm x 30.5 cm) art paper behind pattern pages and cut patterns out to produce two copies. (Or pattern can be cut out and then traced and recut on the art paper.)

3. Place a tongue depressor or popsicle stick between the patterns and glue the two pieces together. Allow the stick to extend enough to make a comfortable handle.

4. Use an X-acto knife to cut eyeholes in each mask (figs. A, B, C, and D).

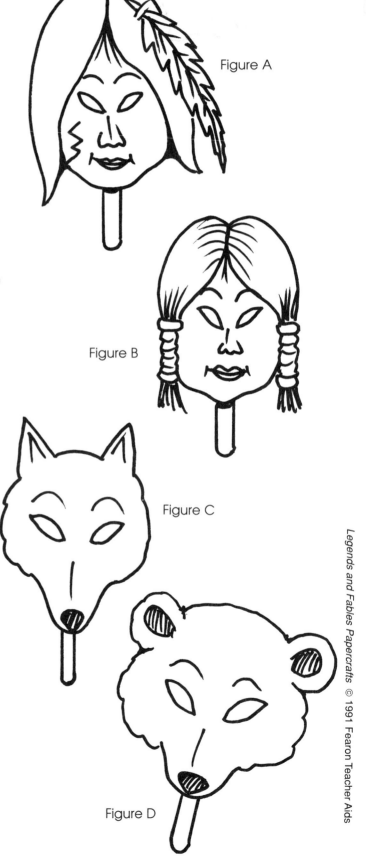

Figure A

Figure B

Figure C

Figure D

Legends and Fables Papercrafts © 1991 Fearon Teacher Aids

The Legend of Scarface (Scarface Mask) 41

The Legend of Scarface (Singing Rains Mask)

Legends and Fables Papercrafts © 1991 Fearon Teacher Aids

The Legend of Scarface (Wolf Mask)   43

The Legend of Scarface (Bear Mask)

The Legend of Scarface (Owl and Savage Bird Stick Puppets)

Materials

- Patterns on pages 46-47 reproduced on white art paper
- White art paper 9" x 12" (22.9 cm x 30.5 cm)
- Tongue depressor or popsicle stick for each puppet

Procedure

1. Color patterns using crayons or markers.

2. Place white art paper behind pattern pages and cut patterns out to produce two copies. (Or patterns can be cut out and then traced and recut on the white art paper.)

3. Place a tongue depressor or popsicle stick between the patterns and glue the two pieces together. Allow the stick to extend enough to make a comfortable handle (figs. A and B).

Figure A

Figure B

The Legend of Scarface (Owl Stick Puppet)

The Legend of the Indian Paintbrush
(Native American)

The Legend of the Indian Paintbrush
(Watercolor Sunset)

Materials

- White art paper 9" x 12" (22.9 cm x 30.5 cm)
- Watercolor paints
- Paintbrush
- Water container
- Native American designs on page 50

Procedure

1. Wet paper generously with clear water.

2. Apply yellow watercolor paint to the lower third of the paper. Continue working upwards on the paper, applying orange to the middle third and then magenta to the top third. Work quickly before the water dries.

3. When all the colors have been applied, hang the paper from the yellow end, allowing the paint to run and blend.

4. Place the paper flat to dry.

5. While the sunset is drying, use white art paper to draw and cut out teepee shapes.

6. Color the teepees and add designs (fig. A).

7. Glue the teepees on the dried sunset (fig. B).

Figure A

Figure B

Happiness
Unlimited

Friendship

Butterfly

Alertness

Rain Clouds

Good Omen

Horse

Deer Tracks

Permanent
Home

Protection

Human Life

Big Mountain

Courtship

Carefree

Wise • Watchful

Temporary Home

Sunrays
Happiness

Peace

Legends and Fables Papercrafts © 1991 Fearon Teacher Aids

The Legend of the Indian Paintbrush (Native American Designs)

The Legend of the Indian Paintbrush
(Paintbrush and Poppies)

Materials

- White art paper 9" x 12" (22.9 cm x 30.5 cm)
- Watercolor paints
- Paintbrush
- Water container

Procedure

1. By using different brush techniques, a beautiful paintbrush flower and poppy can be made. To make a paintbrush flower, fill the brush with paint.

2. Lay the side of the brush on the paper and gently pick it up. Repeat many times placing the prints close together until the paintbrush flower begins to take shape.

3. Add a stem and small sprigs or leaves shooting off the stem using the tip of the brush (fig. A).

4. To make the poppy, fill the brush with paint.

5. Place the brush on its side on the paper. Hold the handle of the brush so it is off the paper. Gently roll the brush to make a fan-shaped design with the paint. Repeat for each poppy.

6. Add stems and leaves using the tip of the brush (fig. B).

Figure A

Figure B

Legends and Fables Papercrafts © 1991 Fearon Teacher Aids

The Town Mouse and the Country Mouse (Aesop's Fable)

The Town Mouse and the Country Mouse (Stick Puppets)

Materials

- Patterns on pages 54-55 reproduced on white art paper
- White art paper 9" x 12" (22.9 cm x 30.5 cm)
- Tongue depressor or popsicle stick for each puppet

Procedure

1. Color patterns using crayons or markers.

2. Place white art paper behind pattern pages and cut patterns out to produce two copies. (Or patterns can be cut out and then traced and recut on the white art paper.)

3. Place a tongue depressor or popsicle stick between the patterns and glue the two pieces together. Allow the stick to extend enough to make a comfortable handle (figs. A, B, and C).

Figure A

Figure B

Figure C

Town Mouse

Country Mouse

Legends and Fables Papercrafts © 1991 Fearon Teacher Aids

The Town Mouse and the Country Mouse (Stick Puppets)

The Town Mouse and the Country Mouse (Dog Stick Puppet)

The Fox and the Stork (Aesop's Fable)

The Fox and the Stork (Fox and Stork Jointed Puppets)

Materials

- Brass fasteners
- Patterns on pages 58-59 reproduced on art paper

Art Paper (Stork):
- White 9" x 12" (22.9 cm x 30.5 cm)

Art Paper (Fox):
- Brown 9" x 12" (22.9 cm x 30.5 cm)

Procedure

1. Color the pattern pieces or add details with crayons or markers.

2. Cut out patterns. Patterns can be glued to tagboard to give them more stability.

3. Stick brass fasteners through the designated holes to connect the pattern pieces (figs. A and B).

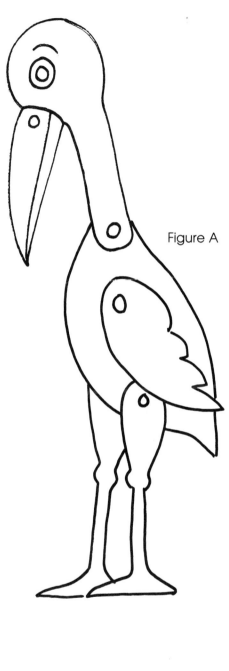

Figure A

Figure B

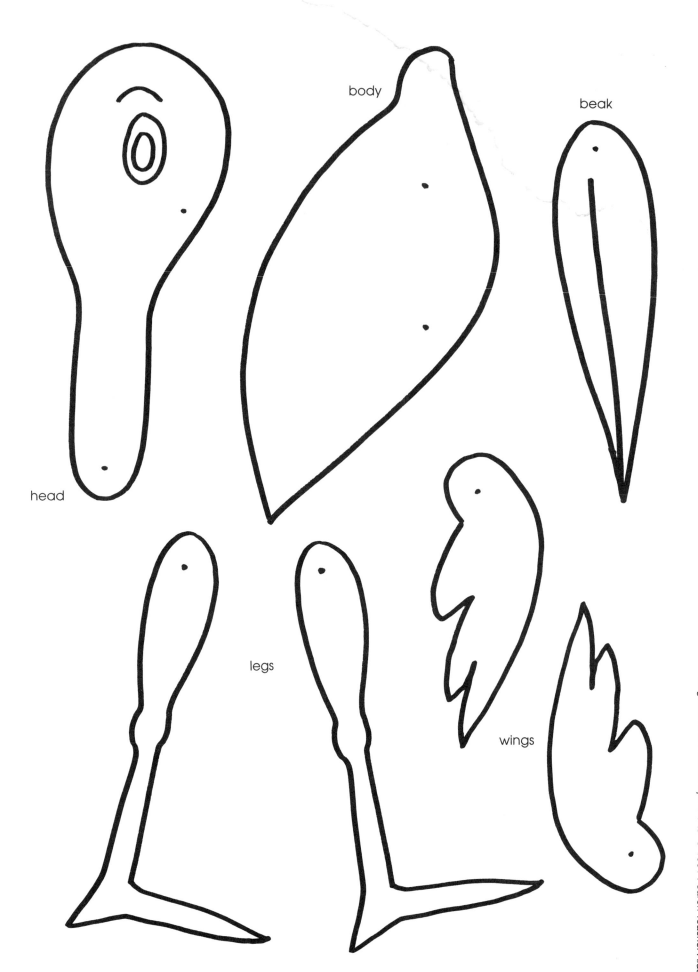

body

beak

head

legs

wings

The Fox and the Stork (Stork Jointed Puppet)

body

head

hind legs

tail

front legs

The Ant and the Grasshopper
(Aesop's Fable)

The Ant and the Grasshopper (Headbands)

Materials

- Stapler
- Tagboard 2" x 24" (5.0 cm x 61 cm) head-band for each insect pattern
- Patterns on pages 62-64 reproduced on art paper

Art Paper (Grasshopper):

- Two green 9" x 12" (22.9 cm x 30.5 cm)

Art Paper (Ant):

- Brown or red 9" x 12" (22.9 cm x 30.5 cm)

Figure A

Procedure

1. Color the pattern pieces or add details with crayons or markers.
2. Cut out patterns and glue grasshopper pieces in place (fig. A).
3. Glue insect in the center of tagboard strip.
4. Staple the tagboard strip to form a headband (figs. A and B).

Figure B

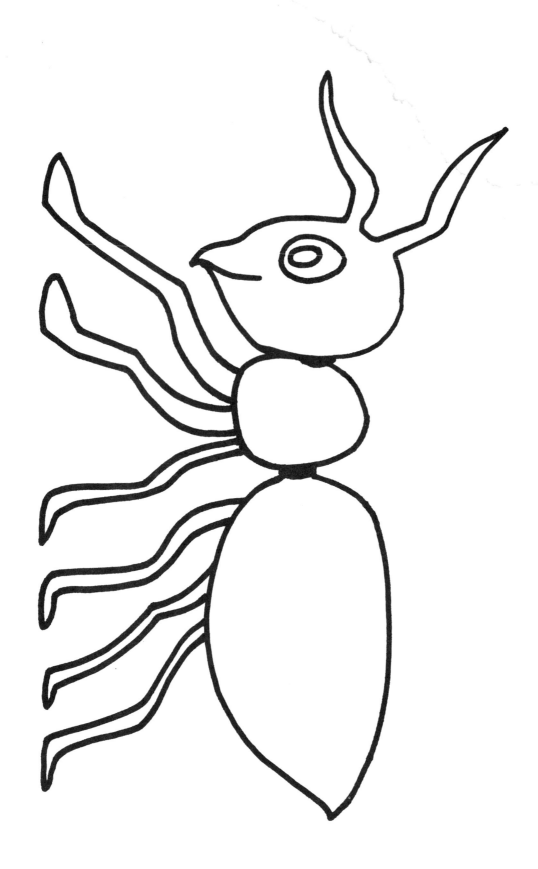

The Ant and the Grasshopper (Ant)

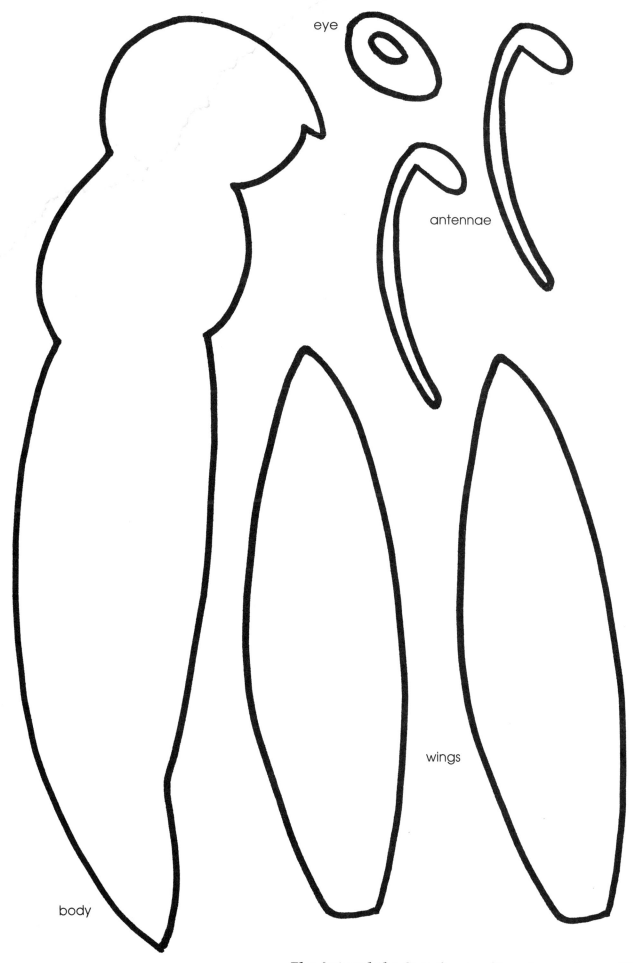

eye

antennae

body

wings

The Ant and the Grasshopper (Grasshopper)

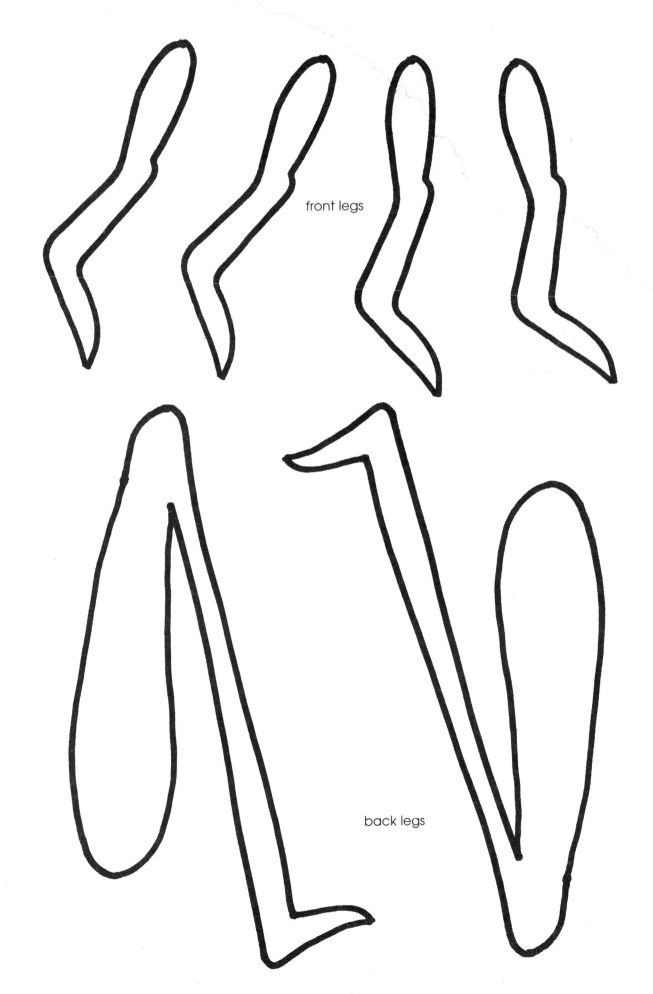

front legs

back legs

The Ant and the Grasshopper (Grasshopper)

Legends and Fables Papercrafts © 1991 Fearon Teacher Aids